The Christian Leader's Wish List

Bill Faris, MPC

Copyright © 2012 by Bill Faris
ISBN-13: 978-0-9834516-8-6

All rights reserved. The authors retain international copyright. Written permission must be secured from the publisher to use or reproduce any part of this book, except for brief quotations in critical reviews or articles.

Printed in the United States of America
Published by Coaching Saints Publications
www.coachingsaints.com
Layout, cover design: www.webvisiongraphics.com

All Scripture quotations, unless otherwise indicated, are taken from the Holy Bible, New International Version®. Copyright © 1973, 1978, 1984, 2011 International Bible Society. Used by permission of Zondervan. All rights reserved.

This book is dedicated to Christian leaders of all kinds, all ages, and all ethnicities. May you be sustained and empowered by amazing grace to glorify God, serve His cause, love His people, and to "run long and finish well!"

Acknowledgements

I would like to thank Kris Miller, Coordinator of the Vineyard Pastoral Sabbath Retreats, and my fellow PSR team members who serve leaders so selflessly over the course of these events. I would also like to thank Mark Fields for including me in the wonderful leader care outreaches provided through Vineyard Missions.

I am grateful to Dr. Steve and Linda Bagley and my Christian counseling associates at Marriage and Family Matters Counseling for their friendship and camaraderie in providing excellent counseling care to our clients, including Christian leaders.

I would also like to thank Charles Bello and the people at Coaching Saints Publications for believing in and supporting this project. And, finally, I want to acknowledge my debt to Dr. Tad Blackburn for the excellent insights on the process of transition that informs the material on that topic in this book.

Bill Faris, MPC
Coto de Caza, California

Table of Contents

Introduction 1

I Wish I Could Find Stress Relief 3

I Wish I Could Develop Satisfying Relationships 15

I Wish I Could Prioritize Personal Development 25

I Wish I Could Thrive Through Transition 35

I Wish My Marriage and Family Could Be Renewed .. 45

I Wish I Could Run Long and Finish Well 55

Introduction

This is, you might say, a love letter to Christian leaders. If you are a pastor, church staff member, missionary, church planter, ministry leader or other person who is fulfilling a call to Christian leadership at either a professional or non-professional level, I am writing with you in mind.

As a fellow Christian leader I understand how rewarding and miraculous our calling can be. However, I am well aware that Christian leadership comes with its own set of taxing and perplexing challenges and personal demands. My hope is that you will find this book helpful in bringing you some timely encouragement and truly useful tips. Should you wish to follow up with more personal contact, you can do so online at the Internet sites listed below.

The six items on this wish list were inspired by my own experiences as well as by my many years of dialogue with other Christian leaders. They have to do with the issues of stress relief, more satisfying relationships, personal development, thriving through transition, marriage and family renewal, and the satisfaction of a well-lived life. Of course, there are other topics that could easily qualify for a "Christian leader's wish list". However, I chose these subjects because of their universal appeal. Who knows? Maybe a *Wish List, Volume II* will follow!

In the meantime I sincerely hope you will enjoy *The Christian Leaders' Wish List*.

William T. "Bill" Faris, MPC
www.ICounselChristians.com
www.BillFaris.com

> *Note: The names used in the personal examples are not those of the actual individuals portrayed.*

Chapter One
"I Wish I Could Find Stress Relief"

Andrea was feeling stressed out and overwhelmed and it bothered her that she couldn't seem to just shake it off. As an experienced Christian leader, missionary, wife, and devoted mother, she had learned to cope with many kinds of challenges over the years. She and her husband had faithfully poured themselves into their roles as leaders of an overseas ministry training base with much good fruit to show for their efforts. Many young people had been trained for Christian service and local churches were being strengthened, too. Andrea even helped lead efforts to address some of the tough social issues in their part of the world. In general, Andrea would say she lived a rewarding life, and yet she found herself struggling with discouragement and depression that was beginning to sap her strength and disrupt her peace of mind. She needed someone to talk to. As it turned out, that someone was me.

Through our interactions I learned more about the highs and lows of her Christian leadership experience. She told me about what she called her "life in the churn"—a term she used to describe the comings and goings of leaders, friends, and workers that are typical of a ministry training environment. Although Andrea had been trained to anticipate "the churn" phenomenon, she and her husband found the particular demands of their leadership roles to be endlessly challenging. In addition, her commitment to the well-being of her children had lately been requiring Andrea to make tough new choices about the re-balancing of her various roles, responsibilities and resources.

Another factor that was testing Andrea at a new level had to do with a particular spiritual emphasis that had begun to find wide acceptance among her friends, leaders and co-workers. While there were many things about this emphasis she could affirm, Andrea observed that it was producing the troubling side effect of reducing their level of commitment to the hard work of the ministry. This left her feeling alone, overtaxed, misunderstood and discouraged. It was her hope that our work together could help her regain her equilibrium and negotiate the various challenges she was facing.

You may not be a missionary at work on the foreign field but, as a Christian leader, you have your own set of unique stresses, dreams, obstacles and opportunities. In order to run long and finish well you will need to manage these factors effectively. This will not be possible, however, unless you can find useful ways to handle the stresses that go with your particular ministry lifestyle.

Stress relief, then, is not a *luxury* for Christian leaders but a *necessity*. The burdens and demands of leadership can weigh on us until burnout, depression, self-defeat and other symptoms of mega-stress reach a critical stage. That's why it is important for you to adopt some helpful de-stressing attitudes and behaviors. In order to do so, you will need to understand the fundamental mechanisms of stress relief. This will enable you to customize and implement your own methods and reap the benefits.

The good news is that stress relief is as simple as 1, 2, 3. In other words there are just three simple things you must change in order to de-stress. They are:

    1. Your environment
    2. Your rhythms
    3. Your level of stimulation

Let's look more closely at these three factors, beginning with environment.

Changing Your Environment

Even small and simple shifts in your environment can provide at least some stress

I Wish . . .

---

relief. I refer to these minor adjustments as *micro-changes*. In addition, you will find that *mini-changes* and *maxi-changes* in your environment are also helpful. So let's briefly review these three categories of environmental change (micro-, mini-, and maxi-) and note some of their characteristics and benefits.

A *micro-change* in your environment can be as simple as leaving your office or other work-associated place for a few minutes in order to shift your mental focus. For example, I will sometimes leave the hard walls and enclosed space of my counseling office to go outside and momentarily enjoy the simple water fountain that is a part of our office complex. Standing near the fountain enables me to treat myself to a micro-environmental change. The sound of the splashing water and the lively spray provides a welcome alternative to the static spaces of my indoor surroundings. In this simple way, I am able to shed at least some of the accumulated stress I have picked up that day. Other micro-changes may include scheduling an appointment or meeting at a local coffeehouse, park or other location. One pastor I know conducts nearly all his casual meetings at the local Starbucks. You can try taking a short walk or engaging in some other gentle physical activity that allows for at least some small change of scenery.

A *mini-change* is a step above a micro-change. It involves changing your environment for at least a few hours and moving to a space that has even less of an association to your workspace than a micro-change allows. A mini-change offers you a complete break from your usual leadership burdens and mental focuses. This might include taking a drive through the country, a walk on the beach, a stroll through a mall, an afternoon nap or some other similar change of pace and scenery. The goal of a mini-change is not to simply find a different place from which to do your work. It is about giving yourself an actual break from your work long enough for you to return to your responsibilities later with a refreshed perspective.

A *maxi-change* represents an even more extensive change in your usual work and responsibility-related environment. This can be as grand as a pre-planned family vacation or as modest as a 48-hour personal retreat. There are two keys to achieving a maxi-change. One is that there is absolutely nothing in your environment that connects to your normal ministry life or responsibilities. The other is that you are able to experience yourself apart from your ministry role or roles. This is you being you and nothing more. A maxi-change allows you to unhook from your leadership roles, labels, and responsibilities in order to simply *be*. For a little while you are not the pastor, the missionary, or the ministry leader. You are yourself as a child of God. Period. When was the last time you enjoyed that feeling?

Changing Your Rhythms

The second change you can make is in your life rhythms. These changes come in two forms:

- Inserting rhythms of refreshment where they did not formerly exist
- Altering your present rhythms to be more efficient and effective

By inserting new rhythms of refreshment into your schedule, you can build spaces for stress relief into your day, your week and your lifestyle. Notice how God built rhythms of rest into the lives of His people, Israel. The Hebrews were called by the Lord to observe a weekly Sabbath, various annual feast days, a year of rest for the land every seventh year and, of course, a designated "Year of Jubilee" every 50 years. Notice how these rhythms are spaced into both short and long term cycles. Like the biblical nation of Israel, we too need variations in the rhythms of our lives as well.

Perhaps the first place to begin thinking about inserting a new rhythm would be to add a weekly Sabbath rest. Of course, for many Christian leaders, the day of the week that serves as a "Sabbath day" for others is actually a "work day" for them. Even annual holidays such as Easter and Christmas are filled with extra activity for Christian leaders. Therefore, you will need to be creative when it comes to inserting alternative spaces into your schedule. In short, you need to design and observe your own personal Sabbath time.

Personal Sabbath

A personal Sabbath is not simply a day off from work. Rather, it is a recurring and regular time and space that is set apart from all other responsibilities as holy to the Lord. It is sacred space that allows your heart, mind and body to be truly present to God, to your family and to your own personal development and renewal.

A personal Sabbath involves both a *disengagement* from your usual duties and responsibilities and an *intentional engagement* with the Spirit of God. It also includes meaningful time for yourself and the most important people in your life. Your Sabbath represents a holy rhythm that is set apart from all the other rhythms of your life. Although it is true that establishing a habit of daily devotions and prayer can be very helpful, a personal Sabbath should consist of a minimum of at least one-half of a day set entirely apart from

I Wish . . .

your normal routine. This space in time can be made available to personal Sabbath activities such as spending time with family, enriching personal reading and prayer, some recreational activities, and so on. And, by the way, sitting in front of a TV and zoning out for hours is not a Sabbath-worthy endeavor!

Other rhythms of refreshment include regularly scheduled retreats, personal appointments with a counselor or spiritual director, spending time with a "Power of Four" group,[1] engaging in refreshing recreation, physical activity or exercise, a "mini-moon" with your spouse, and so on. A number of these alternatives will be described in more detail a little later.

Finally, altering your life rhythms involves harmonizing your responsibilities with your natural peak cycles of functioning whenever possible. If you are a "morning person," for example, you will ideally be tackling the most stressful and demanding things you face before lunch. The "afternoon tiger" or "night owl" will seek to apply themselves to their most demanding challenges during their particular peak periods of productivity. To fight these natural rhythms is both distracting

---

[1] The Power of Four is discussed in more detail in the next chapter.

and draining. Working with these cycles, however, is far more productive and empowering.

Changing Your Levels of Stimulation

The third factor you can change in order to achieve stress relief is to alter the types and levels of stimulus to which you are exposed. As human beings, we have been created and equipped by God to respond to stimulation. Add to this the fact that our environment trains us to automatically respond to certain prompts or signals. Overstimulation and constant stimulation both increase our stress factors by continually keeping us in a mode of hyper-engagement and reactivity.

On a physical level, this has a lot to do with the presence of adrenaline and other chemicals in our body. Emotionally, we all know that leadership and ministry come with built-in demands, relationships, and responsibilities that keep us in high gear. And when it comes to our spirituality, the habit of being still before the Lord and receptive to His presence can easily be lost in the buzz of a given day. Add to this the fact that it is easier than ever to "juice" our system with caffeine or other chemicals any time we please and it's no wonder so many of us feel like we are operating on the ragged edge. Sadly, this hyperactive treadmill of overstimulation has taken many a Christian leader out of the sweet spot of their calling either temporarily or permanently.

Slow Down and Breathe Deep

As an alternative to the nearly constant levels of stimulation that go with people-work, we Christian leaders need to develop spaces and habits that allow us to reduce our exposure to the over-stimulating pulses in our environment throughout a given day. An easy way to do so is to practice breathing deeply and more slowly. The goal here is to take a moment to stop what you are doing, sit quietly, and breathe deeply and slowly by utilizing so-called "deep cleansing breaths." (Those of us who took childbirth classes will recognize this technique!)

We begin by drawing in a breath through our nose and filling our lungs to capacity with the air we take in. As we let this breath out through the mouth we can slow our minds and shed distractions. Feel them leave you along with the exhaled air to float away forever. In conjunction with this deep breathing, we simultaneously set our minds on the Lord (Isaiah 26:3; Colossians 3:2) and on the presence of the Spirit of God who lives within our very bodies (I Corinthians 6:19-20).

Christ-centered and intentional deep breathing invites us to loosen stresses and burdens and also clear the decks of our minds and souls for a few moments each day. I have found it helpful and effective to combine deep cleansing breaths with the slow and deliberate recitation of the Lord's Prayer (or "Our Father," see Matthew 6:9-13). I combine a few words of the prayer with a breathe-in/breathe-out pattern that causes me to slow down and meditate on the meaning of the words Jesus taught us. By doing so, I am able to become more aware of the Father, His kingdom and His glory.

Yet another pause that refreshes is to combine this same breathing technique with thoughtful and specific expressions of thanksgiving. For example, I like to take a moment at several points throughout the day to stop and take at least five deep cleansing "thank you" breaths. As I exhale each time, I make it a point to focus on a different reason for my gratitude to God. Each exhaled breath is a simple prayer of thanksgiving.

Of course, there are many other legitimate ways to release our minds and souls from the constant bombardment of overstimulation. The key is to find several that work for you and to then build them into your daily practice. You will also want to plug some practices into your other life cycles. By reducing your levels of stimulation along with changing your rhythms and shifting your environment, it is possible to successfully de-stress

I Wish . . .

---

and, as a result, live in a way that allows you to be more present to the things that truly matter to you and to God.

Chapter Two
"I Wish I Could Develop Some Satisfying Relationships"

Brad was a lonely pastor. It's not that there weren't people in his life. In fact, he was constantly spending time with people! However, there was almost no one he felt he could count on to "be there" for him in the ways he tried to "be there" for others. It was hard to bring up the topic of his loneliness to anyone, including his wife. His attempts to do so seemed to worry and discourage her and the last thing he wanted was to be a burden to her. He also found it difficult to think of sharing his feelings with his peers. After all, he didn't want to come off as weak or needy around his fellow leaders.

Lately, Brad's gnawing loneliness had pushed him to explore sexually edgy Internet sites. While online, he could indulge his fantasies of being attended to by beautiful women. This made him feel more powerful and in control. But, after awhile, these private indulgences also left him feeling guilty and more alone than ever. Who could he talk to? Who could he let inside? With whom could he share his secret fears, aches, dreams, and inadequacies? Could meeting with a Christian counselor help? Were there others with whom he could authentically connect and be real?

Made For Relationship

The Scriptures are full of reminders that we were created for meaningful relationships. Our Creator is Himself a Trinity—One who is in eternal relationship with Himself as Father, Son and Holy Spirit. Created in His image, we too have an inborn craving for deep and satisfying relationships.

Meaningful relationships are those in which we both know and accept others and are truly known and accepted by them. People-work is notorious for denying us the opportunities for such relationships while simultaneously filling our lives with people. The fact is that it is difficult to have relationships in our lives that are not role-related. Perhaps this is why we leaders often experience an ironic malnourishment of soul and poverty of friendships. This, however, need not be the case.

Part of what draws many of us toward ministry is an interior need to be needed. Indeed, few things are more fulfilling in this life than knowing that God has used us to bless or help others in Jesus' name. However, if our service is too deeply rooted in our own emotional needs we will only be able to go so far before running into a wall of personal depletion. Many Christian leaders have told me of their need to find a deeper place from which to serve. This place is one rooted in a sense of God's affirmation of their lives as well as a deep connection to His eternal streams of purpose and calling.

While it makes sense that our lives will be characterized by a commitment to shepherd God's flock, reach the lost, and strengthen believers, we cannot fulfill such a call for very long while simultaneously neglecting our own need for meaningful give and take. Wouldn't it be refreshing if we could enjoy a few safe, deep and profoundly rooted relationships even as we give of ourselves to others? Of course, it would. But how can we develop relationships of this kind?

The Power of One, Two, Three and Four

Deeply satisfying relationships come in a variety of forms. Each has different characteristics. I have categorized these relationships as: *The Power of One*, *The Power of Two*, *The Power of Three* and *The Power of Four*. Let's take a closer look at each of them.

The Power of One is the power of your personal relationship with God. Some refer to this as your "secret history" with God. There is no question that maintaining our primary relationship with the Lord is Job One. This is a matter of personal necessity if we are to thrive in the ministry. In addition, our one-on-one relationship with the Lord is the source of the "saltiness" that flavors our Christian leadership. Only the Lord knows us down to the last detail (Psalm 139). Therefore, He is awaiting us to say yes to a more intimate relationship with Him.

The key factor of this Power of One relationship is integration. This means that our relationship with the Lord has produced congruency and consistency within. Note the way the Psalmist describes his hunger for such a deep personal intimacy with God in Psalm 42:1-2: "As the deer pants for streams of water, so my soul pants for You." The Power of One is about the way we attend to this relationship. After all, without a rich Power of One relationship, it will be impossible to sufficiently nurture the other important relationships of our lives.

The Power of Two is the power of partnership. The scriptures remind us that, in human terms, "two are better than one..." (Ecclesiastes 4: 9). Of course, those of us who are married are meant to find our core life partnership with our spouse. However, the Power of Two also involves

. . . I Could Develop Some Satisfying Relationships

mentoring and support partnerships of other kinds. These may include partnerships with a ministry associate, a counselor, an old friend, a beloved family member, or a handpicked mentor. Who is it that comes to mind when you think of beginning or renewing such a partnership?

The Power of Three is the power of the work team. Three working together on a given task or project can often make greater strides than either a duo or one person working alone. When three come together to focus on a project they find it relatively easy to place the project at the center of their attention. In doing so they are better able to perceive the obstacles and opportunities at hand, which in turn maximizes team effectiveness.

Finally, there is *The Power of Four.* This is the power of *selected companionship*. Jesus modeled this in the way He set Peter, James and John apart from the others in His inner circle for a uniquely close relationship. At times, these four men shared things the other disciples did not experience (see for example Matthew 17:1). A Power of Four relationship, then, is one in which the participants intentionally select each other on purpose. This is not about randomly drawing four names out of a hat. A Power of Four group consists of four men or women who believe that they will truly bring benefit to one another's lives. For this reason, each

I Wish . . .

---

member chooses all the others that will join him or her in the group and agrees to connect regularly with them.

For some years now I have participated in Power of Four groups. I consider them to be indispensible to my spiritual growth, personal clarity, timely inspiration and inter-personal empowerment. In addition, these groups have given me the opportunity to live in humility and honesty on a regular basis. Sharing my important goals, struggles, victories, temptations and life experiences with "my guys" has transformed my character and strengthened my faith. Of course, this can only work when a strict code of confidentiality is maintained. Happily, my Power of Four group values honest and safe relationships. This allows rich wisdom and good feedback to abound.

The sole agenda of our P4 group is to walk with each other in life as brothers in Christ. We are not a task-oriented group per se. We are not trying to get through a book study or solve church or social problems as a think tank. Our purpose in meeting is to listen to one another and be present to what God is doing in each other. When we come together we talk, we laugh, we offer hope, we teach and we disciple one another out of the riches of our relationship with God, the truth of His Word and the lessons of our life experiences. We also regularly pray for one another and hold each other accountable to godly standards as friends and fellow believers.

Too Difficult?

As a Christian leader, you may think a group like this is way out of your reach. We all know that leadership is loaded and taking the risk of interpersonal vulnerability is not easy. However, you should know that developing a Power of Four group of your own is not as difficult as it may seem. That's because you don't need to personally come up with three other candidates for your group. You begin with one. The two of you can team up on selecting a third potential member and then the three of you can join forces to find a fourth. Note that at each point, there must be buy-in from all the other group members. This keeps things safe, comfortable and of high value for all involved.

Once your P4 group is constituted, you will find that it bears some resemblance to a work team (Power of Three). But instead of making a project or task the center focus, one group member at a time receives attention from the others. This sets up a valuable feedback loop that provides a collective "360 degree view" of any issue or topic under focus. This opens the door to life changing insights and personal transformations. One of my P4 brothers puts it this way: "I could not be the man I am today but for the men God has placed in my life".

Other Relationship Constellations

I hope it is clear by now that Christian leaders need some meaningful and vulnerable relationships if they are to thrive in their life and their calling. Indeed, this is one of the secrets to finishing well. These relationships invite us to be fully human. In addition to emphasizing the necessity of a vital and growing relationship with God, we who are spiritual leaders are also called to model healthy human relationships. It is interesting to note that the New Testament includes some fifty "one another" (from the Greek word *allelon*) statements, including: "love one another," "admonish one another," "confess your faults to one another," "bear one another's burdens" and "forgive one another."

In addition to the types of relationships we have noted, the Bible describes several other deeply meaningful interpersonal relationships. Take, for example, the legendary friendship shared by David and Jonathan (I Samuel 18:3) or the unique nature of Peter's relationship with Jesus (John 21:15 and following). A special intergenerational connection existed between young Samuel and Eli, his priestly mentor (I Samuel 3:1-14). And let's not forget the treasured "father-son" relationships the Apostle Paul sustained with his protégés Timothy and Titus (See 1 Corinthians 4:17). Indeed, the scriptures chronicle a wide range of the vital relationships Paul shared with special individuals, couples, families and groups such as his stated affection for the mother of Rufus who was "like a mother to me" (Romans 16:13).

As Christian leaders, we are invited by people to share their most intimate and profound life experiences. We visit the sick and dying. We comfort and pray with their loved ones. We conduct funerals, baptisms, weddings, vow renewals, counseling sessions and baby dedications. We support dedicated single adults, strengthen families in crisis, and speak up on behalf of the marginalized. In short, we provide the "ministry of presence" for others when it really counts. But, when it comes to our relationships with others, how can we be expected to endlessly give away what we do not receive? We need to have a variety of quality relationships if we are going to succeed in offering quality relationships with others. This is the

I Wish . . .

"power" in the Power of One, the Power of Two, the Power of Three and the Power of Four.[2]

---

[2] For more information on the Power of Four or to schedule a presentation on this topic, you are invited to contact the author.

Chapter Three
"I Wish I Could Prioritize My Personal Development"

Over the past couple of years, I have participated in several first-rate leader care retreats as a part of a pastoral care-giving team. These special opportunities have been some of the most meaningful and fulfilling ministry experiences of my life. I love serving dedicated ministry professionals as they take time to invest significantly in their personal development. They tell me how refreshing it is to be able to focus on their personal growth as opposed to their professional development for a change.

Continuing personal development makes it possible for spiritual leaders to effectively engage the endless stream of challenges and possibilities that require their attention. Nevertheless, it is difficult for leaders to make room for personal growth on a calendar already jammed with meetings, responsibilities, crisis management and the daily demands of leadership. Indeed, some leaders feel guilty about taking time for their own renewal and development. The sad outcome of this neglect is a leader who is trying to do more and more with less and less.

Me, 3.0

One of the most obvious measures of the progress of our rapidly changing world can be found in the never-ending parade of new and improved personal technology products. Looking back, I can still recall the "wow" factor of our family's first personal computer. Push a few buttons and—voila!—the Christmas mailing labels were printed out and ready to go! Your PC enabled you to track family finances, store recipes, and print documents. And let's not forget that astounding new word processing capability! Bye, bye typewriter. Hello, miracle machine!

Another technological wonder of my early adulthood was the amazing cassette tape recorder. Although small in size, a compact cassette could store an entire vinyl album's worth of music or other audio information (up to 90 minutes per tape) for replay upon demand. Cassettes could also be mailed across the world or played in an automobile over and over again. Of course, today's MP3 players are smaller than a cassette tape and can hold unprecedented amounts of information. My how things change! No doubt the future will deliver

... I Could Prioritize My Personal Development

even more amazing advances as the technology continues to open doors.

If "constant change is here to stay" then the struggle to keep pace with the constant flow of technological information and overstimulation will be ongoing. If you are like me, all this change can leave you feeling left behind, like a lowly cassette tape in an MP3 world. However, just as changes in technology challenge us to keep stretching ourselves we also have the ongoing need for continued growing on a personal and spiritual level. The fact is that we cannot really afford to check out and stop growing within. Ongoing personal and spiritual growth is what will keep us fresh in our faith and sharp in our skills. Therefore, it is imperative for us to identify strategic ways to maintain our overall development.

A good place to begin is with a simple personal assessment. Even a brief assessment allows a leader to pinpoint the areas of his or her lifestyle and relationships that are most urgently in need of attention. By focusing first on these areas you can maximize your efforts to bring renewal, balance and fruitfulness to your life and ministry.

I have found it helpful to organize a simple self-assessment around the acronym EAR: Engagement, Activity, Rest. We'll use these three touch points as a means of personal assessment in what follows.

Engagement

Growth requires regular engagement with *God*, with *people*, with the *self* and with *life-long learning.*

Of course, the Scriptures call us to engage with God through prayer. We can also engage Him by studying and meditating upon His Word and by opening ourselves to the moving of His Spirit in our lives. These days, a growing number of Christian leaders are discovering the value of practicing long-treasured spiritual exercises such as the *Lectio Divina,* the *Examen* and other intentional practices.[3] These are simple tools that can help us to slow us down and increase our conscious awareness of God's presence in our lives.

- *I would rate the level of my regular personal engagement with God as:*

    ___ *Satisfying* ___ *Mediocre* ___ *Insufficient*

Engaging with people is another key avenue of personal growth, especially when this involves

---

[3] For an excellent introduction to these and other spiritual practices, see *Prayer as a Place,* by Charles Bello (2009, HGM Publishing) and *Sacred Rhythms* by Ruth Haley Barton (2006, IVP Books). Both are available on Amazon.com.

going beyond the reporting level of communication into the sharing of our opinions, our feelings and our dreams, fears, convictions and insights. It is best if this is not haphazard. What if we actually scheduled this kind of interpersonal engagement with others on a regular basis? How about regularly attending retreats, joining with or starting up a Power of Four group, or meeting with a counselor or spiritual director? Imagine how life would be different if we built in space and time for such meaningful interactions with others.

- *I would rate the level of my regular meaningful engagement with the important people in my life as:*

    ___ *Satisfying* ___ *Mediocre* ___ *Insufficient*

Engagement with the self happens through reflection, solitude, journaling, participation in a hobby or recreational activity and other such endeavors. To neglect the self in this sense is not a Christian virtue and is not to be confused with the biblical notion of *denying self*. To legitimately engage the self is to experience our being as a redeemed son or daughter of God.

To engage our self is to raise our awareness of our own uniqueness and of the particular gifts and graces God has given us to manage (I Peter 4:10).

I Wish . . .

One friend of mine imagines that God will ask us at the end of our lives: "Why weren't you *all* the (<u>your name here</u>) I created you to be?" Without thoughtful engagement with the self, it is hard to imagine how we could be everything God uniquely designed us to be for His greater glory.

- *I would rate the level of my regular meaningful self-engagement as:*

    ___ *Satisfying* ___ *Mediocre* ___ *Insufficient*

To be engaged in life-long learning is to remain mentally, spiritually, intellectually and socially renewed. In the past, the idea of "intelligence" was measured solely as a matter of a standardized intelligence quotient (IQ). However, a far more holistic notion of intelligence is gaining ground. Total intelligence is now understood to be a matter of one's EQ (emotional quotient), RQ (relationship quotient) and even SQ (spiritual quotient) in addition to their IQ. Therefore, to engage in life-long learning is to invest intentionally in growing in all of these dimensions of being and function.

- *I would rate the level of my intentional involvement in life-long learning as:*

    ___ *Satisfying* ___ *Mediocre* ___ *Insufficient*

Activity

In addition to the various kinds of engagements we have outlined, we must also consider our need for activity. Please note that I am using the term "activity" instead of "exercise". Exercise is one form of activity, of course, but there are many others.

Activity simply refers to *kinesis* (motion). When viewed in this regard, the amount of activity available to us is limitless. Adding activity is as easy as parking a little farther away from a store entrance in order to put some extra *kinesis* in our day. Or, we might take a moment for a few jumping jacks or stretches between appointments. By taking the stairs instead of an elevator or by riding a bike to run an errand instead of driving a car, we can add constructive activity to our day without skipping a beat.

Adding even small amounts of extra activity to our day increases the potential of greater alertness. A little *kinesis* can elevate our heart rate, improve our mood, break up the day's routines, and even open a door for ministry to others or for fellowship with God. When you consider how much time Jesus spent walking and talking with others in the course of His daily life and ministry on earth you can see how being "out and about" can create new spaces in your life for God and His kingdom. Once you set a goal of adding a little more activity to your day, you can even make a game of discovering new and interesting ways to do so.

- *I would rate the level of my regular daily activity as:*

    ___ Satisfying ___ Mediocre ___ Insufficient

Rest

Having touched on the need for activity, it is now time to remember our need for rest (*non-kinesis*). Practices that quiet the mind, still the body, and rest the soul are needful for those who live a lifestyle of giving to others. I have touched on some of the techniques for achieving rest earlier but I would like to add a couple more for your consideration.

One meaningful way to insert some rest into the day is to catnap. A catnap is a fifteen-minute nap—an afternoon "siesta" if you will—that puts a refreshing break into your day. There are ways to catnap without interrupting your duties in a big way. For example, instead of scheduling several afternoon appointments back-to-back, you might insert a half-hour break between two appointments. During that time you could take a brief nap, pause for some prayer or thanksgiving, and throw in a

. . . I Could Prioritize My Personal Development

little stretching or other activity at the end. This can really put a healthy and refreshing lift into a demanding day.

Another restful practice is to intentionally insert a "let go and let God" moment into your day. You can do this by simply sitting or standing in a comfortable position with your head lifted up so as to focus your thoughts on the Lord. Next, you cup your hands together and imagine that they are filled with specific stress-producing thoughts, concerns, decisions, events and individuals. With your head still lifted, you now lift your cupped hands high as if holding up this collection of concerns to the Lord. There is no need to verbalize very much at this time as your very movements are themselves a prayer. Finally, you part your hands and allow the concerns to spill away from you to be gathered by the hand of God—for Him to hold, lead and manage. You conclude this exercise by holding your uplifted hands in praise and worship to Him in gratitude (Psalms 88:9, 63:4; 28:1).

- *I would rate the level of my regular practice of rest as:*

    ___ *Satisfying* ___ *Mediocre* ___ *Insufficient*

Having now conducted this simple review, take a look at the responses you gave to the self-

I Wish . . .

---

assessment questions in this chapter. Now make three brief comments in regards to what you observe in the space below:

1.

2.

3.

Chapter Four
"I Wish I Could Thrive Through Transition"

When I first met Stan and his wife, I was instantly drawn to them as a couple. Stan had served his church long and well through many ups and downs. His first marriage had concluded in a heart-wrenching divorce. After some time, he got to know a woman who seemed to be a perfect fit for his life stage and ministry vision, as he was for hers. Lana was single, energetic, creative and deeply committed to Christ. She was also enthusiastic about Stan and his calling as a Christian leader. Their marriage launched them into what they anticipated as a fulfilling and fruitful future together. However, following the proverbial "honeymoon phase" of their new union, Stan and his wife began to struggle as a couple. The stresses and strains of their major life transitions were beginning to tax and discourage them. They finally recognized that they needed to reach out for help from someone they could trust. They needed someone who could help them work their way through their transition from one way of life to another.

Transition Time

As we all know, the ministry leadership lifestyle has many built-in transitional seasons. For the missionary, this might include a move across the world followed by an intensive cross-cultural immersion. For other Christian leaders there will be changes in leadership roles, new ministry partnerships, organizational realignments, life-cycle readjustments and so on. Of course, there are times when we choose our transitions and other times when they seem to choose us! But all transitions, no matter what their source, share certain distinct and identifiable phases. They are:

1. **Preparation for Disengagement** (may be short, long, or virtually non-existent)
   In this stage we prepare for the changes to come.

2. **Disengagement** (detachment)
   In this stage we actually engage change. This includes saying goodbye to and releasing the familiar and moving into the actual process of transition toward the "new normal" yet to come.

3. **Transition** (disorientation)
   In this stage we are fully engaged in the process of transition and the often-strong sense of disconnection and disorientation that accompanies deep change.

4. **Preparation for Reengagement**
   In this stage, we are preparing for our reconnection to the "new normal". As in the disengagement stage, this sub-process may be short, long or virtually non-existent.

5. **Reengagement** (reattachment)
   In this stage, we have identified and are living in our "new normal".

Learning how to negotiate our transitions smoothly makes a big difference in our overall well-being. Successful transitions also affect the well-being of our loved ones, the people we lead, our ministry legacy, and a host of other issues.

One of the outstanding transition stories of the Bible is the account of the exodus of the Jewish people from the land of Egypt. After spending some 400 years as slave laborers in the Egyptian world, God sent His people a deliverer in Moses. Moses' call required him to get his oppressed people out of Egypt and, once free of their oppressors, to get the "Egypt" out of them! Each new phase of their post-detachment journey came with a host of new challenges—but isn't this always the case when we engage a major new period of transition?

The Exodus transition was continuously fraught with confrontation, conflict and collapse. By the time the Hebrews entered into the land of promise some 40 years later an entire generation of the Hebrew nation had come and gone. As they began to possess their new homeland, many miraculous signs and wonders attested to the fact that a new era had dawned. However, this time of reattachment was a mixture of shining displays of fearless faith followed by disappointing acts of blatant disobedience. This reinforces the notion that even those transitions brought about by the hand of God can be intensely challenging. As Christian leaders, we may find ourselves wishing for seamlessly smooth transitions and endlessly fruitful new beginnings but this is clearly not always the case.

Grief and Celebration

A process of grief and a process of celebration are the bookends to any cycle of transition. On the front end of change (detachment / disorientation phase) the grief process is in play. Because entering transition includes the loss of things, people, places and reference points that are familiar or comforting, we grieve. Classic models of the grief process often include the following components:

- **Denial**
  ("This is not happening to me." "I can put off engaging this change." "It won't really impact me much." "I won't really miss the old familiar.")

- **Bargaining**
  ("Maybe the change won't really come." "Let's lower our expectations or minimize our needs in order to avoid change." "Maybe a miracle will prevent or delay these changes." "I'll try harder, do more, step it up to keep things the same.")

- **Anger**
  ("It's your fault we have to change." "Why is God asking this of me / us?" "Life is not fair." "I refuse to accept this transition." "I didn't ask for this change so why do I have to undergo it?")

- **Sadness**
  ("I've lost too much." "This is too hard." "I'm not ready for this." "I'm really going to miss this place / these people / this role / this time in my life, etc." "I hate this.")

- **Resolution**
  ("It's not so bad." "God is good—all the time." "I can see the possibilities ahead." "I / we will make do." "This kind of thing has always worked out in the past." "I'll be okay.")

I Wish . . .

Understanding that grief is normal to the process of detachment and disorientation reminds us that the anger, sadness or other grief symptoms we may feel are not permanent. Resolution is coming! Our sense of impending resolution will grow as we complete our journey through the disorientation phase of transition. Once on the other side of this in-between phase, we will begin to reattach to our new situation, new relationships, new identity and new environment. Doing so will increase our sense of relief, resolution and hope for the future.

The season of reattachment brings about the other bookend of the transition process: celebration! This process includes:

- **Discovery**
  ("Look at the possibilities!" "I didn't see this coming!" "This is better than I thought." "God is growing me / us through this change.")

- **Reconciliation**
  ("I can thrive here." "This is different, but it's not bad." "I think God can use this in my life and the lives of others." "I'll make the best of this.")

- **Worship**
  ("Not my will, but Thine be done!" "Glory to You, God, for what you will do in this new season of change." "Look what God did while we weren't

watching!" "Praise God, He's got good things in store!")

- **Thriving**
  ("I never knew this about myself / my gifts / my resilience / my faith until undergoing these changes." "Look at how I've grown!" "I like my new friends / new role / new place / new opportunities.")

- **Celebration**
  ("We made it!" "We've come this far by faith!" "Let's spread the good news!" "Change is fun—I like it!" "Welcome to the new me / us!")

That is why it is important to know where we are on the map when it comes to the transitions we are currently engaging. If we are on the front end of the change process we will likely still be grieving. If so, we must not artificially rush through the grieving or bury it as if it were not important. To do so would be as challenging as forcing a large beach ball to remain beneath us while we paddle in a swimming pool. It takes a great deal of energy to keep grief submerged. And (as in the case of the submerged beach ball) it is likely that our true feelings of anger, sorrow or bargaining may "pop up" for all to see.

It is also vital to understand that disorientation—the middle phase of transition—may either require a relatively short amount of time or a rather long period. You must not rush through this phase either. Many report feeling lonely, sad, confused, full of doubt and somewhat overwhelmed during the period of disorientation. Nevertheless, once you understand that such feelings are to be expected we are able to more properly work with them as you await the reattachment yet to come.

Thriving

To thrive though transition is to roll with the grief process that occurs in the detachment phase as we enter into the wilderness of disorientation. Once there, we can look for God, for it is often in these places of wilderness and disorientation that we most powerfully experience His presence and intervention. It is in this phase, then, that we may experience the most spiritual growth while in transition. If our vision of Christian maturity is one in which things only get better and better as the non-stop blessings pile higher and higher we may fall completely apart while in transition. But if we greet the grief process and wilderness struggle as a unique and powerful opportunity to experience the presence of God, then even our most difficult days will yield good fruit. The One who promises to "never leave or forsake" us is the same God who prepares a table of fellowship for us in the presence of our enemies. It is there, in the valley of death's shadow (Psalm 23:4-5), that we may most powerfully encounter the living God as our shepherd, our portion, and our friend.

To thrive also involves entering into the new in a way that allows us to begin to resolve our grief and kick off a process of celebration. As we experience new identity, productivity, opportunity and reconciliation we find that there is new life awaiting us. This realization brings about a fresh season of worship and rejoicing as we experience the faithfulness of God through times of change once again. Whether you have chosen your season of transition or it has chosen you, remember that you can thrive if you take the time to understand where you have come from, where you are, and where you are likely to be headed as transition uncoils.

You may find it helpful to discuss your transition "map" with a counselor, spiritual director, mentor, trusted friend or other helpful guide.

Chapter Five
"I Wish My Marriage and Family Could Be Renewed"

Arnold and Beth were serious about their marriage, their family and their role as church leaders. Both were highly committed to their pastoral roles and responsibilities and to the people of the church they planted together. Beth, among other things, led the ministry to the women in their congregation. Arnold was responsible for the worship ministry, overall administration and the regular preaching and teaching. Their children were also highly involved in the church and even helped with some of the key ministry programs. Church leadership was, in short, a family affair.

Arnold was feeling more and more concerned, however, that the price of all this dedicated service to others was turning out to be a slow-burning marital and family crisis. He and Beth had little in common outside of the kids and their ministry life. In addition, their lives were full to the brim with various meetings, events, and consuming responsibilities. This left them little time for renewing their core relationship with one another.

Lately, there had been some experiences with their teenagers that caused Arnold concern. Did these family struggles represent the "new normal" for his household? Arnold decided that the time had come for him to begin meeting with a local Christian counselor in order to get some support for himself and for his family before things became unmanageable. He sensed God did not want him to thrive in his ministry only to fail in his home life. He would reach for change while he had the chance.

A Big Price Tag

Arnold and Beth's story is far from exceptional. Many couples and families in ministry will recognize their challenges. The fact that a ministry leadership lifestyle can be uniquely tough on marriages and families is well documented. As someone living a Christian leadership lifestyle you are no doubt familiar with the unique strains on marriages and families that come with professional and non-professional Christian service. Furthermore, it is likely that you have witnessed the tragedy of a leader who has succumbed to these and other family stresses. Many Christian leaders could authentically report the following when it comes to living a Christian leadership lifestyle: "At first it was *ideal*, then it turned into an *ordeal,* and now I want a *new deal*!"

I'm assuming, however, that you truly treasure your call to Christian leadership and that you also care deeply for your spouse and family. You're not seeking a *new deal* as much as you are seeking *renewal*—for both yourself and for your family. You would gladly welcome fresh breezes to blow through your marriage and family life to dispel the slowly gathering gloom of stress, burnout and terminal distraction. What might such renewal look like? A few of my own experiences have provided some clues.

The Three "News" of Renewal

My wife and I are survivors of ministry-induced marital crisis. Although it was years ago, I'll never forget the day when she tearfully reported to me, "Your arms are just not there for me anymore." At that time, I considered myself to be a fully devoted follower of Christ, committed to both ministry and family. Her sad statement shocked me. How could she have not experienced my regard for her? What had I been missing? How could I address her heartache and convince her that things would surely change?

That day, I began to understand that all marriages, including good marriages, need constant renewal. Here are three things that can bring such renewal into your life and your home. They are:

1. A new priority
2. A new message
3. A new set of habits

A New Priority

First, there is the issue of a new priority. My wife and I have always put our own relationship with God above all human connections so as to properly center our lives on Him. Robin has never challenged me to put her above God or to leave the ministry as a test of my commitment to her. Her message to me that day was that I had somehow become so distracted and consumed by my calling, responsibilities and lifestyle that I had stopped affirming her value to me. Somehow, without my realizing it, I had ceased tending to the things that made her feel loved and important.

I took her message to me as a wake-up call. Whether or not I thought she held a proper place in my priorities was not the point. *She* did not feel she did, and that was enough feedback for me to realize that things needed to change. This meant that the time had come for me to reorder my priorities and refresh my focus. I simply could not allow her legitimate claims on my time, attention and affections to be ignored or resented. Nor could

I drift into an attitude that allowed me to take her for granted. So, priority one (after God) would be Robin. The acid test as to whether or not I was succeeding would be the feedback I would get directly from her. I would need to ask her out loud how I was doing at giving her the message of her priority to me and then listen non-defensively to her answer.

Although Robin's wake-up call first came to me years ago, I continue to initiate conversations with her about this issue today. I ask, "Are my arms there for you? Do you feel like I'm putting you at number one after the Lord?" Her answers to those questions keep me in tune with the level of renewal we need to experience as a couple. How would your spouse respond to these questions if you were to ask today?

A New Message

In addition to a renewal of priority there is also a need for the renewal of the messages we send our loved ones. We often send legitimate messages to our spouse and children about the fact that there are ministry-related crisis situations that must be handled. We make no bones about letting them know that there are important meetings we must attend. We insist that our schedules must be shaped around the demands of our role as a

Christian leader. After all, the people for whom we care are the same people who give of their time, talent and treasure so that the ministry can go forward—the same ministry that sustains our family in practical terms. But what are the messages we send to our loved ones that reinforce how important they are to us? Are we regularly sending them messages that we are committed to them? That we value them? That we enjoy them? Such messages give life to our loved ones. I love the way singer-songwriter James Taylor expresses this when he exhorts us in song to: "Shower the people you love with love. Show them the way that you feel."

At one time, I served on the staff of a large church whose senior leader was a master at sending affirming and loving messages to his wife and children while in the midst of his demanding ministry lifestyle. For example, he pledged to his son that, if at all possible, he would never miss a single one of his high school football games. I know of one time that this commitment required him to leave an overseas ministry engagement early in order to get home in time for the Friday night game. Imagine the message his son received from this devoted ministry-minded father! Imagine the message his commitment to his son sent to the church staff and membership about what was

. . . My Marriage and Family Could Be Renewed

important to him as a Christian Leader! This is just one example of a new message sent well.

Other simple ways to send a new message to our loved ones might be to gently surprise our spouse or child with a one-on-one meal out together. Or we might set aside a half hour in our workday for a walk with a loved one. Try brewing a favorite cup of coffee to share together or setting aside time to take in a movie or visit a nearby garden spot. One of my busiest Christian Leader friends recently decided to initiate weekly "date nights" with his wife after over twenty-five years of not doing so. Believe me: she definitely got his new message via the attentiveness he was now showing her. This change in message definitely set their marriage into the direction of renewal.

Recently, my teenage daughter declared Tuesday evenings to be "Ice Cream Tuesdays." After dinner on Tuesdays, we head to the local ice cream shop for a scoop of an old favorite or to sample an enticing new flavor. Or we might make homemade milkshakes for ourselves with some scoops of good ice cream and fresh fruit. By simply agreeing to observe "Ice Cream Tuesdays" with her, my daughter gets the message that her inspirations and ideas matter to me. She also gets the message that time spent solely on her is important to me. Nowadays, hardly a Tuesday

I Wish . . .

morning passes without her alerting me, "You know what day it is today?"

"Yes," I reply. "It's Ice Cream Tuesday!"

Of course, there are more expensive and sophisticated ways to send a new message to your loved ones. I'll never forget the time, for example, that my wife arranged to have me delivered to the airport under false pretenses (thanks to a friend who, as it turns out, is a convincing deceiver). Once there, I was suddenly informed that she was "kidnapping" me for a getaway to our favorite California coastal hideaway! I will never forget the surprise and delight I felt! But whether the means of sending our message is large or small, the important thing is for us to get out of our rut and employ some new ways and means of telegraphing how much we value the people God has given us to love.

A New Set of Habits

The final means of renewal we will examine is a new set of habits. One of the new habits we have adopted in our home involves my cooking most of our dinner meals. I began doing so following a devastating automobile accident my wife endured over a decade ago. Since then, I have chosen to continue shopping for our regular meals and cooking and serving dinner. This habit provides a

... My Marriage and Family Could Be Renewed

simple way for me to serve my family on a regular basis and, in so doing, make their lives better. And, to my delight, Robin insists on cleaning up the dishes afterwards!

Some time ago, I also took on the management of our daily finances and bill paying—something my wife used to do. The time came when I finally recognized that doing so weighed her down emotionally while allowing me to remain detached from the details of our financial condition. About that time, a friend counseled me to ask my wife if she would like me to take on the management of the family finances and bill paying. Robin said yes right away. I'll be the first to admit that I'm not perfect at this job, but over the years, maintaining this once-new habit has really helped my wife understand my commitment to serve her and our family.

Finally, I have developed new prayer habits in regards to my wife and family. While most of us have probably established habits of prayer for our loved ones by now, I would like to suggest some new things you can add to your habits of prayer. For example, at dinner you might try going around the table and each offering one example of something you saw, felt or experienced that day that gave you life. Then, once each person has taken a turn, a prayer might be offered to thank the

Lord for the specific ways in which He has blessed your hearts and fed your souls.

You may wish to write out a brief prayer and leave it as a note under a pillow, in a packed lunch, on their Facebook page, or under the windshield wiper of their car. Or you might try quietly praying for your spouse or child while they are sleeping. (This is one of my personal favorites because I am a light sleeper!) Even if they are not aware of your intercession on their behalf and your blessing of them in prayer, they can still experience the grace-based benefits of your efforts.

Blow, Breezes, Blow!

Renewal of our marriage and family connections is an essential ingredient to ministry longevity. We can see how important this is when we review the Apostle Paul's lists of qualifications for eldership as outlined in his epistles to Timothy and Titus. A number of the items listed there reflect a wholeness and balance that brings integrity to the leadership of an overseeing elder (see Titus 1:5-9, for example). By incorporating new habits, new messages and new priorities in our most important family relationships, we can sow good seed into their lives, our lives, and the kingdom of God.

Chapter Six
"I Wish I Could Run Long and Finish Well"

I'm not sure who first coined the phrase "to finish well" but it brings to mind my friend and mentor, Bob Whitaker (yes, that's his real name). As I write this, Bob is in his eighties. Over the years he has served the Lord as a pastor, an author, a Bible school professor, a speaker, a retreat leader and a mentor to many. It has been my privilege to see in him a prime example of a Christian leader who has run long and is finishing well. This is a true privilege, indeed!

In his book, *The Making of a Leader,* Dr. Robert Clinton records the sober observation that people like Bob are the exception rather than the rule. The sad fact is the majority of leaders—including biblical leaders—actually fail to finish well. But there are five factors, Dr. Clinton asserts, that can make a critical difference to how a Christian leader will complete his or her race. These five factors were gleaned from Dr. Clinton's study of 1,300 leaders. This sampling includes 50 biblical leaders, 100 historic leaders and a large number of contemporary leaders. He lists the five factors as follows:[4]

1. A lifetime perspective
2. Distinct experiences of personal renewal
3. Personal disciplines
4. A posture of learning
5. Mentoring

Let's look at each of these more closely.

Perspective

It is clear that the Apostle Paul's ability to maintain perspective strengthened his ability to persevere, remain focused, and finish well. Not only did the apostle view his present experience in the light of his earthly lifeline, but he also extended his perspective into eternity. "I consider that our present sufferings are not worth comparing with the glory that will be revealed in us," he writes in Romans 8:18.

The wise leader understands that suffering goes with the territory of their call to spiritual leadership. But it is also understood that one's own

---

[4]

https://docs.google.com/a/vcmn.org/viewer?url=http://www.impactleader.org/articles/wp-content/uploads/Finishing-Well-Five-Factors-That-Enhance-It.pdf suffering must be placed within the context of the eternal glory that awaits those who endure to the end.

> *"Now there is in store for me the crown of righteousness, which the Lord, the righteous Judge, will award me on that day—and not to me only, but also to all who have longed for His appearing." (2 Timothy 4:8)*

Such a perspective will strengthen us in times of reversal and temptation. It gives us the power to endure the difficulties of this life for the sake of the life to come.

Another gift of perspective is the way it helps us to be less likely to judge ourselves unrealistically. It is easy to fall into the trap of comparing our lifestyle or leadership abilities with others. Such comparisons may lead us to judge ourselves as inferior, or even cursed! However, an informed and scriptural perspective reminds us that worldly measurements are not capable of revealing the true quality of our contribution to the lives of others. The fact is that our true impact is a secret known only to the Lord. It is information that will not be available to us until we stand before the judgment seat of Christ (Romans 14:10). Until then, faithfulness must be at the core of our definition of success.

Personal Renewal

Not long ago, I had the privilege of working with an unforgettable couple while serving as a pastoral counselor on a ten-day retreat. At the start of our time together, the wife shared some deep concerns about her husband. Specifically, she feared that he had gone physically and emotionally "around the bend" due to the magnitude and duration of the stresses they had been facing. Ironically, these stresses were the result of the ultra-rapid growth of the church they led.

My own attempts to connect with her emotionally spent husband at the beginning of the retreat were strained. His ability to carry on an extended social conversation had dropped to a minimal level. He had little affect or emotion and was a bit robotic in his social manner. I can honestly report that I have rarely seen anyone as comprehensively depleted as this dedicated leader appeared to be.

After several days of soaking in the abundant opportunities the retreat provided for personal, marital, spiritual, emotional and physical renewal I began to witness a most remarkable change. It was like watching the arrival of springtime after a long, dark winter. By day five it was as if another man was beginning to emerge from behind the mask of exhaustion. This "thaw" continued over the remainder of our time together. It was simply amazing to watch him smile readily, tell stories, and interact warmly with others. He and his wife were coming alive as a couple, too. They had been enjoying the opportunities the retreat provided to go on walks together and participate in some of the other recreation opportunities that were offered.

Day-by-day I watched as he heartily participated in the times of worship and showed interest in the daily teaching topics. Personal prayer and counseling ministry topped off the life-giving renewal in progress. The replenishment was unmistakable. I would summarize my observations of this couple's transformation as follows: they had been so busy *doing* that they had forgotten what it meant *to be.* They are by no means alone.

As profound as this transformation appeared to be, their shift would only be sustainable if they could successfully incorporate new practices into their lifestyle back home. The retreat introduced them to these new spiritual practices, rhythms and habits including some simple and effective ways to meet one-on-one with the Lord on a personal level. They also learned the vital importance of taking time for deep rest and of connecting more intimately with others they could trust. The challenge would be for them to plug into these skills and changes once they returned home.

Before leaving the retreat they made specific plans to reorder their routine so as to include their newly acquired spiritual habits and the life-giving rhythms of rest and recreation. About a year later, I was able to get a follow up report from the wife. She reported that the changes they had made were holding and working well. Furthermore, she joyfully shared her relief that she truly "had her husband back" after fearing that she had lost him to ministry burnout forever.

In order for it to really take root and bear fruit, the renewal of leaders must be comprehensive in scope. Attention must be paid to not only personal and spiritual habits but also to the marital, recreational, emotional and interpersonal dimensions, too. This is the kind of renewal that equips a leader to run long and finish well. I wonder: has it been a while since you took some time out for such renewal? What would it take for you to reorder your lifestyle and relationships in life-giving ways at this time? Perhaps a little bit of coaching might help here.

Discipline

Referring to the Apostle Paul's high view of personal discipline, Dr. Clinton comments:

I concur with Paul's admonitions to discipline as a means of insuring perseverance in the ministry. When Paul was around 50 years of age he wrote to the Corinthian church what appears to be both an exhortation to the Corinthians and an explanation of a major leadership value in his own life. We need to keep in mind that he had been in ministry for about 21 years. He was still advocating strong discipline. I paraphrase it in my own words: **"I am serious about finishing well in my Christian ministry. I discipline myself for fear that after challenging others into the Christian life I myself might become a casualty"** *(1 Corinthians 9:24-27).*

One of the most compelling reasons for leaders to live a disciplined life is their propensity to reproduce in kind. A disciplined leader is more likely to avoid the grief that goes with undisciplined living, of course. But he or she is also less likely to reproduce undisciplined disciples!

Many of us feel that we are not, by nature, disciplined people. We may wonder, therefore, whether we can learn the disciplines necessary for a strong finish. It is reassuring, at such times, to think of the young adults as they begin their first phase of training at a military boot camp. No matter how much discipline they may or may not possess upon arrival, these soldiers-in-the-making will soon discover their ability to be more disciplined than they ever thought possible! Perhaps it has something to do with the "motivational gifts" of those legendary drill sergeants! It just goes to show that anyone can learn discipline under the right conditions.

A Posture of Learning

The third of Dr. Clinton's "finish well factors" is the commitment to being a life-long learner. We all know that knowledge is more plentiful and easily accessible than ever, but it requires a certain attitude adjustment if one is to take the posture of a life-long learner. No matter how far along we may have come in our maturity and growth, our final graduation from this life's school of leadership will not come until we go to be with the Lord. "A student is not above his teacher," Jesus said, "but everyone who is fully trained will be like his teacher" (Luke 6:40). Our curriculum, then, is to become more and more like our teacher, Jesus Christ, until we stand before Him on the day when we shall at last "know even as we are known" (I Corinthians 13:12).

Learning, of course, has to do (in one sense) with the accumulation of new data. In this regard, we are living in a time when data is more plentiful than ever. Indeed, it can be overwhelming! A good learner will find his or her own way to sort data, summarize findings, and expand their understanding. But, of course, learning is more than the accumulation of knowledge. For while quantities of knowledge are more available to us than ever, it often seems that the ability to turn this available knowledge into practical wisdom is becoming rare!

A tried and true method for gaining wisdom (and not just knowledge) is through the telling of stories. In particular, leaders can learn a great deal about the potentials and pitfalls of leadership by immersing themselves in the stories of other leaders. This is something that Dr. Clinton has modeled well for us. His study of the lives of leaders has yielded rich insights and many lessons. We would do well follow his example of looking closely at the lives of leaders for the lessons we might learn and apply from their experience. We can do this by reading, speaking with leaders, and by other intentional means of exposing ourselves to their life lessons and personal insights.

Another kind of learning that is vital to the life-long learner is the ability to become the student of one's own experiences. This is where it can be most helpful to keep a journal or other chronicle of one's insights, experiences and life lessons. I confess that I am not, by nature, attracted to the keeping of a regular journal. Nevertheless, I have found that by keeping a bound blank-paged journal book nearby, I can consistently update it with a few notes on a consistent basis. Over time, I have captured a useful record of my own experiences, prayers, thoughts, observations and goals. These notes truly help me to reflect, review and focus as I travel the path before me. There is certainly no need to waste one's own life lessons these days when we have so many ways available to capture and reflect upon them.

Mentoring

It has been noted that finishing well as a leader is as much about what a person becomes as what they accomplish. The influence of others has much to do with the kind of leader we will become. From our earliest childhood days we learn and develop as we pattern the lives of those we admire. Although the means by which we do so will certainly change over time, there is no substitute for the kind of learning that comes by interpersonal observation and interpersonal mentoring. We might call this life-on-life learning—the kind of development that can only come as one person's life interacts directly with another. The spirit of this life-on-life learning can be found in Paul's words to the Romans when he writes:

> *"I long to see you so that I may impart to you some spiritual gift to make you strong— that is, that you and I may be mutually encouraged by each other's faith." (Romans 1:11-12)*

Mentoring, however, is not only a matter of getting life-on-life with those ahead of you in the race. A complete mentoring constellation includes meaningful interaction with peers who are running alongside you as well as with those who are coming up after you in leadership. Each of these aspects of mentoring includes their own personal growth and development benefits. In other words, there are some things you can only learn as you mentor others and other things that will become a part of you as you assume the role of the mentoree.

You will likely have a variety of mentors throughout your life and leadership experience. Some will be chosen by you, and others will more or less choose you. Either way, we can learn much from our mentors as they share their wealth of experience, personal insights and knowledge over time. A good mentor is someone with whom you can communicate openly, share your struggles, report your victories, pose your questions, and call upon in challenging times. The best mentors are those who invite you to simply hang out with them as they do what they do well. Consider how the Lord Jesus modeled this for us in the life-on-life mentoring relationship he shared with His apostles. Indeed, this was part of Jesus' plan for them. "He appointed twelve—designating them apostles—that they might be with Him" (Mark 3:14). The mentor who takes a personal interest in your development, effectiveness, and strong finish is offering you a gift of almost infinite value.

Peer mentors also make valuable contributions to our leadership development and general well-being. In the give and take of the peer relationship, we both *learn from* and *teach* those with whom we share the road. As in the case of all mentoring relationships, we must select our peer mentors carefully. The ability to keep confidences, emphasize a spirit of advocacy, and provide a base of support is key to the selection of a peer mentor. I have found some of my most relevant and useful resources through my peer mentors, and they would probably say the same of me.

Run Long, Run Well

So, let's review: your prospects of running long and finishing well will be greatly enhanced by maintaining a lifelong perspective, engaging in distinct times of personal renewal, adopting truly useful personal and spiritual disciplines, maintaining a posture of lifelong learning, and interacting with significant mentors, peers and mentorees. Imagine how good it will feel to "break the tape" that separates this life from the glory that awaits us knowing that we are finishing well. Imagine the prospect of hearing the words of our Savior:

"Well done, good and faithful servant! You have been faithful with a few things; I will put you in charge of many things. Come and share your Master's happiness!" (Matthew 25:23)

Conclusion

I hope that this booklet has provided you with some useful tips and tools, personal inspiration and helpful information for your journey as a Christian leader. My prayer is that it will serve as a hand held out to you from a colleague who is interested in helping you run long and finish well—and better enjoy the journey along the way! If there is anything I can do to more personally assist you, please feel free to contact the author as follows:

Email: Bill@mypastoralcounselor.com
Websites: www.ICounselChristians.com,
www.billfaris.com

About Bill Faris, MPC

Bill has spent a lifetime relating to church leaders and pastors. He has over thirty years experience as a Christian leader who has served in large and small churches and as a church planter.

In 2000, Bill expanded the scope of his ministry after receiving his Masters Degree in Pastoral Counseling. Since then he has joined the Christian Counseling ministry of Marriage and Family Matters Counseling in Mission Viejo, California where he sees individuals and couples for counseling by personal appointment. At the same time, Bill maintains church leadership roles in Southern California.

Most recently, Bill has pursued opportunities to participate on teams specializing in providing intensive care for pastors on retreat. On these teams, he utilizes his background in counseling, marriage support, teaching, deep healing prayer and personal coaching to strengthen Christian leaders.

Due to the unique combination of Bill's training and experience, Christian leaders of many kinds have found him to be a trusted ally in their pursuit of their personal and spiritual health and in their quest to fulfill their ministry call.

Bill and Robin, a gifted nurse and professor of nursing, have been married 35 years and have four children ranging in ages from the mid-teens to over thirty years old. His oldest son, Christopher Faris, is also a part of the team at Marriage and Family Matters.

Other Books and Writings By Bill Faris, MPC:

- *How Healed Do You Want to Be?* (Ampelon Publishing, 2009)
- *The Sinkhole and the Mountain* (Available from the author or Amazon.com, 2010)
- *Homegrown: Our First Steps in Bringing the Church Back Home* (Available from the author or Amazon.com, 2011)
- *Gracelets,* a weekly free e-newsletter, is available by writing Bill Faris at: Bill@mypastoralcounselor.com

Other Books By Coaching Saints Publications

From the Sanctuary to the Streets: Insights and Adventures in Power Evangelism
By Charles Bello and Brian Blount
(Available in paperback and electronic book formats)

From the Sanctuary to the Streets is a practical guide written to propel the reader into a lifestyle marked by intimacy with God and power evangelism. Through teaching and personal stories, the authors share with humor and honesty their own efforts to embrace the empowering activity of the Holy Spirit. As the authors state, "We are not called to be spiritual recluses or trail blazing burnouts. Rather, we are called to be friends of God who live a life of intimacy and impact as we simply do life with God in a naturally supernatural way."

Learning to Suffer Well
By Peter Fitch, D.Min
(Available in paperback and electronic book formats)

Learning to Suffer Well is an interactive devotional study designed to help you think through some of the Bible's teaching about how to face suffering in different situations. It is meant to force you to interact with ideas from the Scriptures in such a way that you will be challenged to grow as a Christian in terms of understanding, honesty, behavior, attitude, and level of spiritual maturity.

The Re-Imaging of God
By Dr. Richard Clinton
(Available in paperback and electronic book formats)

In *The Re-Imaging of God*, Richard Clinton takes us on a journey to explore the ways we perceive God. Our image of God affects every aspect of our lives and our leadership. It is paramount that we begin the adventure to understand our images of God and re-image God based on Biblical images of God. Filled with personal examples, thorough study and reflection questions, Clinton guides us in our endeavor to re-image God.

Prayer as a Place: Spirituality that Transforms
By Charles Bello
(Available in electronic book formats)

Prayer as a Place is an invitation to partner with Christ as he leads the believer into the dark places of his or her own heart. The purpose of this journey is to bring holiness and wholeness to the child of God. With candor and brutal honesty, Pastor Charles Bello shares his own reluctance and then resolve to follow Christ on this inward journey. In sharing his story, readers gain insight into what their own personal journeys may look like. *Prayer as a Place* reads like a road map as it explores the contemporary use of contemplative prayer as a means of following Christ inward.

Recycled Spirituality: Ancient Ways Made New
By Charles Bello
(Available in electronic book formats)

Recycled Spirituality is like browsing through a mysterious, ancient resale shop filled with treasures from the rich heritage of historical Christianity. Many of the ancient spiritual disciplines have continued to be in use for thousands of years—others are being newly rediscovered. These classical disciplines are drawn from our shared Catholic, Orthodox, Protestant, Evangelical and Pentecostal traditions.

Recycled Spirituality is written as a practical handbook to encourage and equip readers to push the borders of their own experience and personal faith traditions to encounter God in fresh ways. The purpose of these encounters is always transformation, renewal and missional living. As Charles writes, "The gift of tradition is meant to be received. The essence of tradition is meant to be rediscovered. And if the practice of a tradition helps form you into the image of Christ, it is meant to be recycled."

You can order these books and additional copies of *The Christian Leader's Wish List* by visiting our website at www.coachingsaints.com.

www.ingramcontent.com/pod-product-compliance
Lightning Source LLC
Chambersburg PA
CBHW060348050426
42449CB00011B/2867